EXPLORE BLACK HISTORY with WEE PALS

by Morrie Turner

Copyright Morrie Turner, 1998 Creators Syndicate. All rights reserved. No part of this book may be reproduced or utilized in any form or by any means, electronic or mechanical, including photocopying recording or by any information storage and retrieval system without permission in writing from the publisher. Inquiries should be addressed to JUST US BOOKS, INC. 356 Glenwood Ave., East Orange, NJ 07017

Printed in Canada/ First Edition 10 9 8 7 6 5 4 3 2 1

ISBN: 0-940975-79-3

CONTENTS

Richard Allen	2	James Farmer	16	Thurgood Marshall	30	James M. Trotter	45
Naomi Anderson	3	Thomas T. Fortune	16	Benjamin E. Mays	31	Sojourner Truth	46
Crispus Attucks	4	James Forten	17	Kweisi Mfume	32	Harriet Tubman	47
Ida Wells Barnett	5	Henry Highland Garnet	18	Constance Baker Motley	33	Nat Turner	48
Daisy Bates	5	Dick Gregory	19	Huey Newton	34	UNIA (Universal Negro Improvement Association)	49
Mary Frances Berry	6	Francis James Grimké	19	Odetta	35	Robert L. Vann	50
Mary McLeod Bethune	7	Fannie Lou Hamer	20	Rosa Parks	36	David Walker	51
Julian Bond	7	Frances E. W. Harper	20	Adam Clayton Powell, Jr.	36	Booker T. Washington	52
H. Rap Brown	8	Josiah Henson	21	P.B.S. Pinchback	37	Walter White	52
Linda Brown	8	Benjamin Hooks	22	Benjamin Quarles	38	George W. Williams	53
Joseph Cinque	9	Charles H. Houston	22	Paul Robeson	39	Margaret Bush Wilson	54
Mary Ann Shadd Cary	10	Charlayne Hunter-Gault	23	Jackie Robinson	40	Carter Woodson	55
Septima Poinsette Clark	10	Roy Innis	24	Bayard Rustin	41	Richard Wright	56
Angela Davis	11	Jesse Jackson	25	Bobbie Seale	42	Malcolm X	57
Frederick Douglass	12	John Jones	25	Dr. James McClune Smith	42	Whitney Young	58
W. E. B. DuBois	13	James Weldon Johnson	26	Althea Simmons	43	Zeta Phi Beta	59
Medgar Evers	14	Coretta Scott King	27	Mary Church Terrell	44	About Morrie Turner	60
Myrlie Evers	15	Martin Luther King, Jr.	28	Kwame Toure	44	Meet WEE PALS	61
		John Lewis	29				

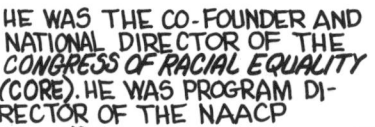

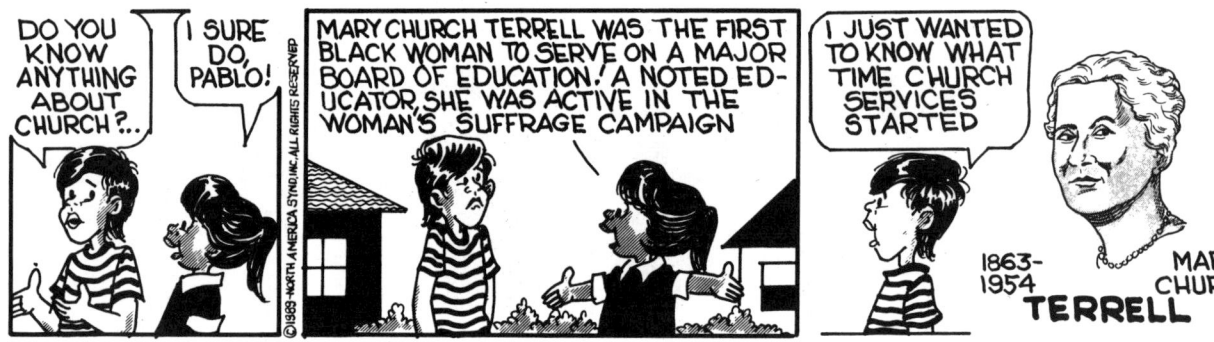

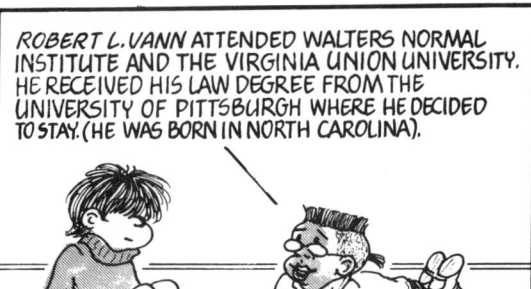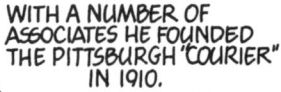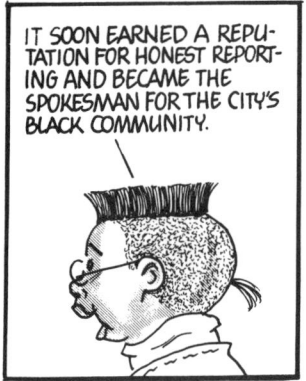

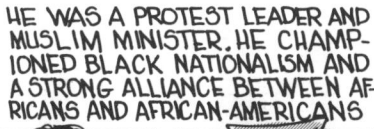

About Morrie Turner

Morrie Turner created the "Wee Pals" comic strip in 1964. Appearing first in *Ebony* and *Black World* magazines, it soon became the first comic strip featuring a multi-ethnic cast of characters to appear in metropolitan daily newspapers. These character sketches were often drawn from actual people in Morrie's neighborhood. "Wee Pals" was adapted into an animated television show called *Kid Power* in 1972.

Morrie Turner has received numerous awards for his comic strip including the B'Nai Brith Humanitarian Award, the Boy's Club Image Award and the California Educators Award. He lives in Berkeley, CA. where he often visits schools, libraries and community groups.

HAVE YOU READ THESE TITLES PUBLISHED BY JUST US BOOKS?

_____	**AFRO-BETS ABC Book** by Cheryl Willis Hudson	$3.95
_____	**AFRO-BETS 1 2 3 Book** by Cheryl Willis Hudson	$3.95
_____	**AFRO-BETS First Book About Africa** by Veronica F. Ellis	$6.95
_____	**AFRO-BETS Book of Shapes** by Margery W. Brown	$3.95
_____	**AFRO-BETS Book of Colors** by Margery W. Brown	$3.95
_____	**AFRO-BETS Kids: I'm Gonna Be** by Wade Hudson	$6.95
_____	**AFRO-BETS Book of Black Heroes from A to Z**	$7.95
_____	**Annie's Gifts** by Angela Medearis/Anna Rich	$6.95
_____	**Baby Jesus Like My Brother** by Margery Brown/George Ford	$7.95
_____	**Jamal's Busy Day** by Wade Hudson/George Ford	$6.95
_____	**Land of the Four Winds** by Veronica F. Ellis/Sylvia Walker	$6.95
_____	**Singing Black** by Mari Evans/Ramon Price	$4.95
_____	**Many Colors of Mother Goose** by C. W. Hudson/K. Brown, M. Corcoran & C. Johnson	$10.95
_____	**When I Was Little** by Toyomi Igus/Higgins Bond	$6.95

Just Us Books ISBN prefix is 0-940975. These titles are available wherever you buy books, or you may copy this order form and mail your order to JUST US BOOKS, INC. 356 Glenwood Avenue, East Orange, NJ 07017
973-672-7701.
Website: JUSTUSBOOKS.com

Please send me the books I have checked above. I am enclosing $ _____ (Please add $2.00 for first book and 50 cents for each additional book to cover shipping and handling.) Send check or money order only, no cash please.

Name
_____

Address
_____

City _____ State _____ Zip _____

Telephone _____

Please allow 2 to 3 weeks for delivery. Offer good in USA Only. Prices subject to change. 22498/JUB